D0067225

BE
UNSTOPPABLE

HOW TO CREATE THE
LIFE YOU LOVE

FOREWORD BY

JACK
CANFIELD

**DAVID
MELTZER**

CYNTHIA
KERSEY

For details about the work of Unstoppable Foundation, please visit UnstoppableFoundation.org.

Foreword

by David Meltzer

Bankruptcy, my lawyer advised. The word reverberated in my mind. *How had my life come to this?*

For years, the "SaaS" company I started had grown exponentially, to over 150 employees — activity which, by age 35, brought my net worth to over $100 million. I owned a golf course, a ski resort, and 33 other properties. And the business had provided my family with an enviable lifestyle of expensive homes, first-class travel, luxury cars, and private schools for my three beautiful daughters.

We had it all, I thought.

In fact, at the time, I saw my successful company as the crowning achievement of a life that had seen me move from one success to another as an Internet entrepreneur, chief executive of the world's first smartphone, and eventually CEO of Leigh Steinberg's global sports agency— the inspiration for the movie *Jerry Maguire.*

So how had it all come crashing down on me?

When had I stopped, as my mother used to say, "living above the line"—that point of control where one crosses over from accountability for one's actions to blame and justification, all while surrounding myself with the wrong people and the wrong ideas?

As I looked back over my life, I began to form a mental list of the life principles and business strategies that had helped me build my success. I realized that I had lived (but forgotten) four key values: gratitude, forgiveness, accountability and effective communication.

I had to forgive myself, become accountable for my actions again, and effectively communicate a new vision for my business that would inspire clients, bankers and others to work with me.

But *gratitude,* I decided, would be the overarching mandate of my life. Instead of being concerned about myself, I would wake up every morning and pray to God to put ten people in front of me whom I could help. I would shift my business paradigm and be of service instead. While that didn't mean I'd stop being a capitalist, *it did mean* I was going to elevate others as I provided value—knowing that I was creating a void for the Universe to fill. If all I did was ennoble and empower and encourage others, I believed, not only would I be able to manifest everything I desired—and by elevating others I would elevate myself.

I wrote a book and began speaking at conferences and teaching others. By relentlessly reapplying these four core values, I rediscovered how important it is for all of us to be in consistent, persistent pursuit of our potential.

When Cynthia Kersey, founder of Unstoppable Foundation, contacted the new spin-off company I'd started with Hall of Fame quarterback Warren Moon, I discovered a new way to help others passionately pursue their own futures. Cynthia was building schools and empowering entire villages in Eastern Africa with clean water, local medical services, and nourishing food. At the time, she'd helped over 35,000 children get an education and had equipped 75,000 people in the Masai Mara to better their lives.

I immediately knew I could help, and was inspired to create a leadership center, so those 75,000 people could cause a ripple effect—changing their society's consciousness and creating empowering, new beliefs in others. Today, my personal and business network is joining me in raising over $1 million to build a leadership training center in Laila, Kenya.

What could you do, once inspired, by consistently, persistently pursuing your potential? If you provide the vision, this book will tell you how.

Introduction

One of the greatest myths in this world today is that we're entitled to live a great life. That somehow, somewhere—someone—is required to fill our lives with continual happiness, enticing career options, empowering family time and blissful personal relationships simply because we exist on this planet. We expect these things—and when they don't show up, for many of us at least, it's someone else's fault.

But perhaps the greatest truth in this world—and the one lesson we hope this book will help you learn over and over again—is that there's only one person responsible for the life you enjoy here.

That person is YOU.

If you want to be successful, you have to take 100% responsibility for everything you experience in your life. From the level of your achievements to the results you produce, to the quality of your relationships to the state of your health and physical fitness—even responsibility for your feelings, your income, your debts...everything!

This is not easy.

In fact, most of us have been conditioned to blame something outside of ourselves for the parts of our life we don't like. We blame our parents, our bosses, our teachers, our friends, our co-workers, our clients, our spouse, the weather, the economy, our astrological chart, our lack of good golf clubs—anyone or anything we can pin the blame on. We never want to look at where the real problem is—ourselves.

There is a wonderful story that is told about a man who is out walking one night and comes upon a man down on his knees looking for something under a street lamp. The passerby inquires as to what the other man is looking for. He answers that he is looking for his lost key. The man offers to help and gets down on his knees and searches for the key. After an hour of fruitless searching, he says to the man, "We've looked everywhere for it and we have not found it. Are you sure that you lost it here?" The other man replies, "No, I lost it in my house, but there is more light out here under the streetlamp."

How many times do you look for the answers to your problems outside yourself, when the answer lies within? It is you who creates the quality of the life you lead and the results you produce. No one else!

Choose Now to Make a Change

Our admonition to you as you start down your path to future success, is that you have control over just three things in your life—the thoughts you think, the images you visualize and the actions you take. How you make the most of them determines the outcomes you experience in life.

If you don't like what you are producing and experiencing, choose now to change your responses. Change your negative thoughts to positive ones. Change what you daydream about. If you don't like the way people treat you, say something about it or spend your time with different people.

If you keep doing what you've always done, you'll keep getting what you've always gotten. In fact, if what you are currently doing was capable of producing the "more" that you are seeking in life, the "more" would have already shown up. If you want something different, you're going to have to do something different!

The day you begin to do that is the day your life will begin to change for the better.

Change Your Thinking and Start Changing Lives

Is there one instance in your life when you made a major change for the better? Better yet, is there a time when that one decision helped changed *other people's lives* for the better? Our good friend and coauthor of this book, Cynthia Kersey, is the Founder of Unstoppable Foundation. She decided to change her thinking and ended up changing lives instead.

When Cynthia and her husband of 20 years separated, Cynthia's pain over the impending divorce opened the door to her greatest purpose. That Christmas, for the first time ever, she and her son traveled alone to her parents' house in Florida. She felt devastated and overwhelmed, but somehow—in the midst of her pain—she made a promise to herself that the next Christmas would not find her so forlorn.

Instead, she would dedicate herself to doing something for someone else.

Looking for advice, Cynthia called her friend and mentor, Millard Fuller, who had founded Habitat for Humanity International more than thirty years before.

"When you have a great pain in your life,' he said, "you need a greater purpose."

Fuller shared with Cynthia his recent visit to Nepal — one of the poorest nations in the world—and suggested that building a house for a Nepalese family in need could be a great project for her.

Would just one house be enough to overcome the pain I'm feeling? Cynthia wondered. *Or would it take more than that?*

Though she had never built even *one house* in her life, it wasn't until the idea of building 100 houses felt big enough to drive away the pain and give her a new purpose in life. Yet at $2,000 per house in building costs, it was a crazy, audacious goal that Cynthia had no idea how she would achieve. She had no connections to big donors and didn't know exactly where Nepal was, but the idea of helping 100 families establish a home of their own kept her energized.

Within a year, by asking everyone she came in contact with to donate, Cynthia achieved her goal of raising $200,000 and brought a team of 18 people to Nepal that New Year's holiday to construct the first of the 100 houses that would ultimately be built over the following year. That trip changed her forever.

Five Simple Steps, One Big Transformation

Today, having worked with countless thousands of villagers, volunteers and change agents in the countries served by Unstoppable Foundation, Cynthia and her implementation partners have greatly expanded their work and honed a five-pillar solution to the desperate poverty they find there.

Education   Healthcare   Nutrition

Clean Water   Income Training

Your purchase of this booklet helps continue the tremendous work that Unstoppable Foundation is doing around the world. (Visit UnstoppableFoundation.org.)

Could you, too, make a change in your thinking and start changing lives—starting with your own? We know you can.

In fact, Cynthia's favorite "success principle" is detailed in *Chapter One* of this booklet. Get started reading on the next page and watch your life become unstoppable!

Chapter One:

Take 100% Responsibility for Your Life With E+R=O

Bob Resnick, one of Jack's earliest mentors, teaches a simple, yet powerful formula we believe should be the primary rule guiding your successful life:

$$E + R = O$$

Event + Response = Outcome

Stated succinctly, every outcome we experience in life is a direct result of how we respond to an individual event that occurs.

Sometimes that event is an unexpected opportunity that shows up. Other times, it's a crisis we didn't see coming. But in any case, it's just the way things are—the existential reality of our life.

So how can we create the best possible outcome in relation to an event we have no control over? By taking responsibility and changing the way we respond to that event. Take a look at these two examples:

Event: You are given a $1,000 bonus.
Response: You spend it on a weekend trip.
Outcome: You are broke.

Event: You are given a $1,000 bonus.
Response: You invest it in your mutual fund.
Outcome: You have an increased net worth.

Can you see how your response—and your response alone—can significantly improve your life, or alternatively, keep you exactly where you are today?

Successful people know that how they respond can mean the difference between advancement and riches — or regret about what could have been. In fact, one of the greatest differences between successful people and those who would merely like to be, is how they respond to the opportunities in their life.

How often have you reacted with fear or "I can't" when opportunity knocks? Have you ever walked away from a life-changing opportunity? Or worse, did you fail to recognize and respond to opportunity that actually appeared as a crisis or other disaster in front of you?

Take a look:

Event: Your co-workers continually miss deadlines, forcing you to work late to bring projects in on time.

Response: You grumble to your wife, but say nothing to your co-workers or boss.

Outcome: You end up working late most nights, straining your marriage and family relationship.

Event: Your co-workers continually miss deadlines, forcing you to work late to bring projects in on time.

Response: You investigate ways to streamline the process, then quietly present your better plan to the boss.

Outcome: Your boss creates a special job title for you, giving you more oversight on projects, which leads to increased responsibility, a year-end bonus and an increase in salary.

The truth is...when confronted with a negative event, successful people look for ways to transform that negative into an opportunity for achievement and greater success.

They simply respond differently.

Do You Blame Events for Your Outcomes?

Responding differently means you must give up blaming the event itself. This is very difficult. Our conditioning has trained us so that when something doesn't work, we blame what happened rather than our reaction to it: the traffic that made you late for an important meeting, the bounced check that made your husband mad, your parents who still treat you like you're 12, the company take-over that eliminated your job.

Does this sound familiar?
"If only my boss would give me enough time to do the job...If only my husband understood what I'm trying to do with the kids...If only the kids would clean up their rooms...If only we had a better economy...If only they would stop such-and-such...I would feel better."

Stop blaming and complaining!

Understand that the E's (the events) aren't responsible for the O's (the outcomes) you experience in life.

Complaining Simply Means You
Know There's Something Better

Complaining about the Events won't help you change your outcomes, either.

Isn't it interesting that many people who stay in bad situations never complain. Why? They simply don't know any better. They don't know that things could be better.

But complainers know exactly what's available to them.

In fact, when you hear someone complain, what they're really saying is, "I know things could be better. I have a point of reference of something better which I prefer. I know the difference between that ideal and the situation I'm in now. But I'm not willing to risk creating that other, more desirable scenario."

It's simply easier and less risky to complain.

And it's certainly easier than responding the way successful people do. If successful people don't like the situation they find themselves in, they either:

(a) work to make it better, or...

(b) they leave and go somewhere else.

The truth is...for as fast as our society moves today, things are likely to change anyway. Left alone, bad situations often get worse. But you can do something to change them—if you're willing to take 100% responsibility for your life. It's up to you to do something different.

Do You Ignore the Yellow Alerts?

Most people are surprised to hear that they're usually notified in advance about the "negative" events that occur in their lives. Like the "yellow alerts" in the old Star Trek television series, you receive advance warnings—in the form of tell-tale signs, comments from others, gut instinct, your intuition—that warn you of impending doom and give you time to prevent disaster from happening.

You have time to change your response (R) in the E+R=O equation.

You can act, as successful people do—facing facts squarely, doing the uncomfortable, and taking steps to change the outcome. Successful people don't wait for disaster to occur, and then blame something or someone else for their problems. They respond in time. They prevent things from going too far.

Life Becomes Much Easier

Once you begin responding decisively to signals and events as they occur, life becomes much easier. The feelings of hopelessness and lack of control go away. You start seeing two kinds of improved outcomes—both internal and external.

Old internal dialogs like: *I feel like a victim. I feel used. Only bad things happen to me,* are transformed into, *I feel better. I'm in control. I can make things happen.*

External outcomes like, "Nobody comes to our store. We missed our quarterly goals. People are complaining the new product doesn't work," become outcomes like: "I have more money in the bank. I lead the division in sales. Our product is flying off the shelves."

Eventually, as you respond regularly to these yellow alerts, you begin to see events without needing these advance warnings. You begin to anticipate problems.

And, you mature in your thinking.

Finally, you can accept the fact that *you* are the one who has created the way things are. You took the actions, you thought the thoughts, you created the feelings and you made the choices that got you to where you are now.

You are the one who ate the food. You are the one who stayed in that job that you hate. You are the one who married him. You are the one who wanted kids. You are the one who abandoned your dream. You are the one who ignored your intuition. You are the one who decided to go it alone. You are the one who decided you were damaged goods. You are the one who trusted him.

And, come to think of it, you're the one who said yes to the dogs, too.

It was you!

You Either Create It or Allow It to Happen

You alone have the power to make something happen in your life, whether you actively create it or passively allow it to happen or continue. This goes for outcomes that are both good and bad.

When you confront a guy in a bar who is twice your size and say to him, "You're ugly!"—then find yourself in the hospital with a broken jaw—It's easy to see you created that outcome.

But what about those outcomes that are more difficult to see?

Let's say you work late every night. You come home tired and burned out. You eat dinner in a stupor, then sit down to watch television. You are too tired and stressed out to do anything else—like go for a walk or play with the kids. This goes on for years. Your wife asks you to talk to her. "Later," you say. Three years from now you come home to an empty house and find note that she's left you and taken the kids.

You created that one, too!

Of course, in this kind of situation, it's easy to gloss over the obvious with self-righteous arguments like, "I was working hard to make a better life for my family. I'm entitled to watch a ball game every now and then. I was a good provider, wasn't I?"

But perhaps the worst outcomes are those we simply allow to happen, whether through inaction, neglect or unspoken agreement.

You didn't sign the petition when it came in the mail, and now there's a microwave tower in your neighborhood. You didn't demand counseling the first time he hit you, and now the abuse has gotten worse. You didn't follow through on your threat to take away privileges, and now the kids' rooms look like a war zone. You didn't go back to school, and now you are being passed over for a promotion. You didn't demand an audit, and now your partner has disappeared with the money. You didn't leave when you saw the drugs, and now you are in jail.

When you allow outcomes like these to happen, be aware that you are not a victim. In fact, you can safely take credit for standing passively by and letting it happen. You didn't say anything, make a demand, say no, or leave.

Like the yellow alerts we talked about before, there were

signs that you chose to ignore.

You didn't acknowledge the alert or act upon it because that would have required you to do something uncomfortable. Whether it's confronting your spouse or speaking up in a staff meeting or leaving the premises, you are the only one who can respond to a yellow alert while there is still time to change it, reverse it or save it.

We like this quote from former Congressman Ed Foreman who once said,

> *Winners are those people who make a habit of*
> *doing the things losers are uncomfortable doing.*

Don't fail to respond to a yellow alert because it's easier, more convenient, less uncomfortable, less confrontational, keeps the peace, doesn't require taking risks, or confirms your low self-image. Take action! Don't allow negative outcomes to be your fate.

Chapter Two:

Decide What You Want in Your Unstoppable Life

One of the most amazing phenomena you'll ever experience as you incorporate these success principles into your daily life is the unexpected phone call, the windfall financial benefit or the uncanny new acquaintance that brings you exactly what you want or need in order to achieve your loftiest goals — almost as if it were planned.

Perhaps it's the Universe, rewarding your new goal-setting activity and take-action attitude by harnessing all the forces at its disposal. Or perhaps you've worked hard and have "grown" yourself to the point where you're finally ready to receive a benefit which had been waiting in the wings all along.

But more probably, as researchers have now come to believe, it may simply be a matter of your subconscious mind focusing on and recognizing opportunity when it arrives.

Whatever the explanation, the reality is that what you want, wants you. Your goals, desires and needs are patiently waiting to gravitate toward you, once you decide what you truly want.

Of course, the main reason why most people don't get what they want is they haven't decided what that "want" is. They haven't defined their goals—exactly—in clear and compelling detail. After all, how else can your mind know where to begin looking, seeing and hearing if you don't give it specific and detailed goals to achieve?

Clarify Your Vision and Your Values

There's a very powerful technique for helping you define your goals in vivid, colorful and compelling detail. But before using this technique to write down your goals...before defining the compelling life you want for yourself, you first must know what your priorities are. Priorities are "wants" that are personally important to you—not those you believe should be important or those you believe the world expects you to value—but what's truly important to you from the deepest place in your heart.

Once you know your "wants," you must also determine your core values. What kinds of activities and priorities are in alignment with your integrity? Which are outside your acceptable limits?

Think about it. You might "want" all the riches and material wealth that could come from selling illegal drugs, but you might find it very difficult to convince your mind and body of your enthusiasm, especially if breaking the law and contributing to broken lives went against your basic values. In fact, engaging in an activity you don't agree with often causes low self-esteem, depression, despondency, even anger. So be sure that what you want matches your values and your life purpose.

Don't Live Someone Else's Dream

Be certain, too, that what you want isn't someone else's version of what you should want.

Jack once met an anesthesiologist who made $350,000 a year, but whose real dream was to work on cars. He had wanted to be a mechanic, but he knew his mother wouldn't approve. Jack's solution? "Give yourself permission to buy a bunch of cars and then work on them on the weekends." What the anesthesiologist wanted in his heart didn't match his picture of what he thought he should be.

Unfortunately, the sad reality for most people is they simply aren't honest with themselves. If they were, they would realize their "want to's" are almost always bigger than their "shoulds."

Make an "I Wants" List

One of the easiest ways to begin determining what you truly want is to ask a friend to help you make an "I Wants" list. Have the friend continually ask, "What do you want? What do you want?" for 10-15 minutes, while jotting down your answers. You'll find the first "wants" aren't all that profound. In fact, most people usually hear themselves saying, *I want a Mercedes. I want a big house on the ocean.* And so on. But by the end of the 15-minute exercise, the real you begins to speak: *I want people to love me. I want to express myself. I want to make a difference. I want to feel powerful*...wants that are true expressions of your core values.

Is "Making a Living" Stopping You?

Of course, what often stops people from expressing their true desire, is they don't think they can make a living doing what they love to do.

"What I love to do is hang out and talk with people," you might say.

Well, Oprah Winfrey makes a living hanging out talking with people. And Jack's friend Diane Brause, who is an international tour director, makes a living hanging out talking with people in some of the most exciting cities in the world.

A woman once told Jack her favorite thing to do was to watch soap operas.

"How can I make a living watching soap operas?" she asked.

Fortunately, she discovered lots of other people loved watching soap operas, too, but often missed their favorite shows because they also had to go to work.

Being very astute, this gal created a little magazine called Soap Opera Digest. Every week, she watched all the soap operas, cataloged the plots and wrote up little summaries, so that if a viewer missed their soap operas that week, they would know who got divorced from whom, who finally married the doctor, and so on. Now, this woman makes a fortune watching and publishing information about soap operas.

See how it's possible to make a great living doing what you want to do? You simply have to be willing to risk it.

Visualize What You Want

Have a friend read this exercise to you or audio-record it and then listen back to it with your eyes closed. Pause about one minute between each of the seven categories.

Begin by listening to some relaxing music and sitting quietly in a comfortable environment.

Then, begin visualizing your ideal life exactly as if you are living it.

1. First, visualize your financial situation. How much money do you have in your savings, how much do you make in income? What is your net worth? How is your cash flow? Next...What does your home look like? Where is it? What color are the walls? Are there paintings hanging in the rooms? What do they look like? Walk through your perfect house visually, using your mind's eye.

At this point, don't worry about how you'll get that house. Don't sabotage yourself by saying, *I can't live in Malibu because I don't make enough money.* Once you give your mind's eye the picture, your mind will solve the "not enough money" challenge.

Simply be honest with yourself about what you truly want. Continue visualizing your perfect home. Next, visualize what kind of car you are driving.

2. Next, visualize your career. What are you doing in your career? Where are you working? Who are you working with? What kind of clients do you have? What is your compensation like? Is it your own business?

3. Then, focus on your free time, your recreation time. What are you doing with your family and friends in the free time you've created for yourself? What hobbies are you pursuing? What kinds of vacations do you take?

4. Next, visualize your body and your physical health, and your emotional and spiritual life. Are you free and open, relaxed, perseverant, in an ecstatic state of bliss all day long. What does that look like?

5. Then, move on to visualizing your relationships with your family and friends. What is your relationship with your family like? Who are your friends? What are the quality of your relationships with friends? What do those friendships feel like? Are they loving, supportive, empowering? Could they be better?

6. What about your own personal growth? Do you see yourself going back to school, taking training, seeking therapy for a past hurt or growing spiritually?

7. Move on to the community you live in and the network you've chosen. It's ideal, isn't it? What does it look like? What kinds of community activities take place there? What about your charitable work? What do you do to help others and make a difference? How often every week do you participate in these activities? Who are you helping?

Write these things down in a journal as you visualize them.

Share Your Vision for Maximum Impact

Then, finally, share your vision with somebody. This can be very uncomfortable. In fact, most people say, "I can't share that! It's too personal. It's too crazy. People will think I'm flaky." But the truth is half the people you talk to will want the very same thing. Everyone wants material wealth, loving relationships, supportive family and friends, and time to help make a difference in our world. But too few of us readily admit it. Sharing your vision helps your subconscious mind become accountable to make it happen.

Cynthia Kersey Shared Her Unstoppable Vision

On a five-day trip to Nairobi, Cynthia attended a women's conference where she met over 400 Kenyan women who had traveled for days to participate and share their plight of poverty, illiteracy, lack of nourishing food, and lack of clean water. These women weren't there to complain. They were looking for solutions to create a better life for their children and their families.

By the end of the conference, Cynthia felt sadness—but also outrage. These people, simply by virtue of where they'd been born, faced back-breaking poverty with little way out.

Please don't forget us, they pleaded to Cynthia and the other *mzungas* (white people) attending. *I promise,* Cynthia vowed.

But how?

Back home, Cynthia learned that a friend's son had asked his bar mitzvah guests to donate money to build a school in Uganda, instead of giving him the typical cash and gifts. At that moment, Cynthia knew how she could make good on her promise to the women in Nairobi.

Since her 50th birthday was fast approaching, she decided to turn it into something meaningful by hosting a party with a purpose. Instead of giving birthday gifts, Cynthia asked friends to join her in giving children in East Africa the gift of education, nourishing food, clean water, and life-saving vaccinations and medical treatment.

One hundred people attended Cynthia's gala birthday party and thanked her for giving *them* the opportunity to make a difference in the world. That night, they contributed $80,000.

What could I do if I really put my time and energy into it? Cynthia thought.

She began to intentionally ask people to join her in her vision. And what she discovered is that people really care. They care about others—in their own communities and half way around the world.

And so they gave.

They held fundraisers. Their children held fundraisers. They asked their friends and network to write checks. They gave up their birthday parties.

And the results have been amazing.

Because of these generous supporters, Unstoppable Foundation has helped educate over 35,000 children and impact over 75,000 men, women and children in the Masai Mara region with its five-pillar model. It's also expanded this work to India so that entire communities are now thriving with the tools to lift themselves out of poverty.

What could YOU do—for your own life and for others—if you shared your vision and recruited others to help you?

Chapter Three:

Stay Focused With the
Total Focus Process

We believe you have inside of you a unique ability or area of brilliance—some one thing you love to do and do so well, you hardly feel like charging people for it. It's effortless for you and a whole lot of fun. And if you could make money doing it, you'd make it your lifetime's work.

Successful people believe this, too. That's why they put their unique brilliance first. They focus on it. And they delegate everything else.

Compare that to the rest of the world who goes through life doing everything, even those tasks they're bad at or that could be done cheaper, better and faster by someone else. They can't find the time to focus on their area of brilliance because they fail to delegate even the most menial of tasks.

When you delegate the "grunt work" — the things you hate doing or those tasks that are so painful, you end up putting them off — you get to concentrate on what you love to do. You free up your time...you're more productive. And you get to enjoy life more.

So, why is delegating routine tasks and unwanted projects so difficult for most people?

Surprisingly, most people are afraid of looking wasteful or of being judged as "above everyone" or of feeling out of control or of spending money. Deep-down, they simply don't want to let go.

Others, potentially you, have simply fallen into the habit of doing everything themselves. *It's too time-consuming to explain to someone,* you say. *I can do it better myself anyway.* But can you?

Determine What You're Brilliant At…
Then Delegate Everything Else

The following exercise is designed to help you determine your areas of profound expertise and those tasks you really should be delegating to others. Keep in mind that you're looking for the *one, two or three activities* that bring you the most money, that bring you the most enjoyment and that you could spend all day doing for free, but that you are so good at, you're paid handsomely by everyone who needs access to your unique abilities.

Step One: List Your Activities and Tasks

Start by listing all those activities that occupy your time…whether they're business-related, personal, or related to your civic organizations or volunteer work. List even small tasks such as confirmation phone calls or copying.

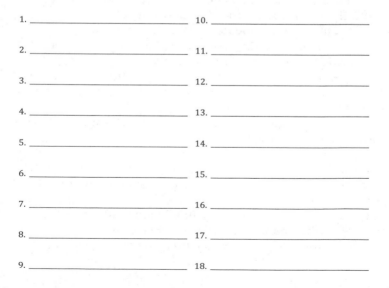

1. _____	10. _____
2. _____	11. _____
3. _____	12. _____
4. _____	13. _____
5. _____	14. _____
6. _____	15. _____
7. _____	16. _____
8. _____	17. _____
9. _____	18. _____

Step Two: Choose Those Activities You're Brilliant At

Next, choose from the previous list those 1-3 things that you are brilliant at, things that very few other people can do as well as you:

1. _____

2. _____

3. _____

Step Three: Decide Which Activities Generate the Most Money

Name the three activities from your original list that generate the most income for you or your company:

1. _____

2. _____

3. _____

Step Four: Determine Where to Focus Your Time and Energy

Identify any individual activities that appear in both short-lists above. In other words, list activities that you are brilliant at <u>and</u> that generate the most income for you or your company. This is the activity or area of expertise where you'll want to focus the most time and energy:

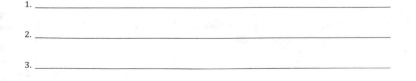

1. _____

2. _____

3. _____

Step Five: Eliminate "Toxic" Tasks

Name any "toxic" tasks from the list on page 22 that you especially dislike doing or that take too much of your time— activities you would gladly delegate to someone else if you could. You'll be transferring these tasks to the Complete Delegation Exercise below:

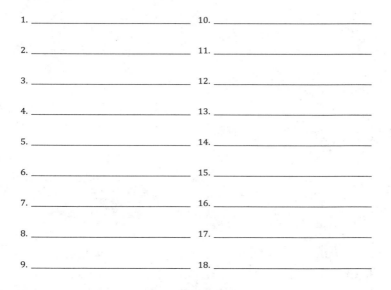

1. _____   10. _____

2. _____   11. _____

3. _____   12. _____

4. _____   13. _____

5. _____   14. _____

6. _____   15. _____

7. _____   16. _____

8. _____   17. _____

9. _____   18. _____

The Complete Delegation Exercise

If you're a professional earning $125 per hour and you pay a neighborhood boy $10 an hour to cut the grass, you save the effort of doing it yourself on the weekend and gain one extra hour when you could profit by $115. Of course, while one hour doesn't seem like much, multiply that by 52 weekends a year and you discover you've gained 52 hours a year at $115 per hour—or an extra $5,980 in potential earnings.

Similarly, if you're a real estate agent, you need to list houses, gather information for the multiple listing service, attend open houses, do showings, put keys in lock boxes, write offers and make appointments. And, if you're lucky, you eventually get to close somebody on a sale.

But let's say that you're the best closer on the planet.

Why would you want to waste your time writing listings, doing lead generation, placing lock boxes, and making videos of the properties when you could have a staff of assistants doing all that and freeing you up to do more closing? Instead of doing just one deal a month, you could be doing a deal a week because you delegated the less profitable activities.

One of the strategies Jack routinely teaches in his seminars is called Complete Delegation. It simply means that you delegate a task once and completely, rather than delegating it each time it needs to be done.

Identify your Area of Brilliance in *Step Four* on page 23, then delegate other tasks in order to free up time to focus on what you love to do.

Chapter Four:

Create a "Breakthrough" Goal That Will Instantly Amplify Your Life and Career

While goal-setting is an important step to becoming more successful, most of the goals we set focus on improving our life in the moment. Get the house painted. Finish my sales report. Clean out the laundry room. Lose 20 pounds.

But what if—instead—you focused on a single goal that would up-level everything you do...from your career to your acquaintances to your income to your lifestyle.

Wouldn't that be a goal worth pursuing with passion? Wouldn't that be something to focus on a little each day until you achieved it?

Think about it.

If you were an independent sales professional and knew you could get a better territory, a substantial bonus commission, and maybe even a promotion once you landed a certain number of customers, wouldn't you work day and night to achieve that goal?

And if you were the coach of a football team, whose typical strategy was to gain 4 yards on every play, what if your players instead worked toward completing a breakthrough 60-yard pass?

If you were a stay-at-home mom whose entire lifestyle and finances would change by earning an extra $1,000 a month, wouldn't you pursue every possible opportunity until you achieved that goal?

That's what we mean by a breakthrough goal. Something that changes your life, brings you new opportunities, gets you in front of the right people and uplevels every activity, relationship or group you're involved in.

For Jack, producing his very first audio program was not only a breakthrough career goal—it became the catalyst that generated $100,000 in extra income per year. Suddenly, as a professional speaker and trainer, he had a product to sell at the back of the room. Soon after, CareerTrack heard the audio recordings and offered to underwrite an entire training program around the material, bringing Jack a substantial royalty. Eventually, Nightingale-Conant reviewed the audio program and offered Jack an attractive contract.

What might your single Breakthrough Goal be? Let the exercise below help you decide.

Breakthrough Goal Exercise

1. Whether *you* believe you can achieve it or not, what *one single change* in your career, business, lifestyle or relationships would boost you to the next level? Is it landing a promotion, meeting a sales goal, changing jobs, expanding your business, finding romance, qualifying for an award, going back to school or some other goal? Write down your breakthrough goal below:

_____

_____

2. Now visualize how your life would change as a result of accomplishing this goal. What would you be doing, seeing and feeling?

_____

_____

_____

Chapter Five:

Take Action on Your Goal By Practicing The Rule of Five

Achieving your Breakthrough Goal (or any other goal, for that matter) can more easily be done by "chunking it down"— breaking down the goal into smaller tasks that you can begin accomplishing in earnest.

But be aware: Preparing to move forward isn't the same as taking action itself.

In other words, preparation, research, planning, getting it perfect...these are all areas where people get bogged down in the "take action" process.

Here's a story from Jack that illustrates this point:

When Mark Victor Hansen and I published the first Chicken Soup for the Soul book, we were so eager and committed to making it a bestseller. We asked 15 best-selling authors ranging from John Gray (*Men Are from Mars, Women Are from Venus*) and Barbara DeAngelis (*Making Love Work*) to Ken Blanchard (*The One Minute Manager*) and Scott Peck (*The Road Less Traveled*) for their guidance and advice. We received a ton of valuable information about what to do and how to do it. Then we visited with book publishing and marketing guru Dan Poynter, who gave us even more great information. Then we read John Kremer's *1001 Ways to Market Your Books.*

After all of that we were overwhelmed with possibilities. To tell the truth, we became a little crazy. We didn't know where to start, plus we both had our speaking and seminar businesses to run.

We sought the advice of Ron Scolastico, a wonderful teacher and guide, who told us, "If you would go every day to a very large tree and take 5 swings at it with a very sharp ax, eventually, no matter how large the tree, it would have to come down."

How very simple and how very true! Out of that we developed what we call "The Rule of 5." This simply means that, every day, anyone can do five specific things that will move their goal toward completion.

With the goal of getting *Chicken Soup for the Soul* to the top of the *New York Times* bestseller list, it meant doing 5 radio interviews, or sending out 5 review copies to editors who might review the book, or calling 5 network marketing companies and asking them to buy the book as a motivational tool for their salespeople, or giving a seminar to at least 5 people and selling the book in the back of the room.

On some days we would simply send out 5 free copies to people listed in The Celebrity Address Book—people like Harrison Ford, Barbara Striesand, Paul McCartney, Steven Spielberg and Sidney Poitier. As a result of that one activity, I ended up meeting Sidney Poitier (at his request). Plus, we later learned that the producer of the television show *Touched by an Angel* required all of the people working on the show to read *Chicken Soup for the Soul* to put them in the right frame of mind.

We made phone calls to people who could review the book, we wrote press releases, we called into talk shows (some at 3:00 in the morning), we gave away free copies at our talks, we sent the book to ministers to use as a source of stories for their sermons, we gave free "Chicken Soup for the Soul" talks at churches, we did book signings at any bookstore that would have us, we asked businesses to make bulk purchases for their employees, we got the book into the PXs on military bases, we asked our fellow speakers to sell the book at their talks, we asked seminar companies to put it in their catalogs, we bought a directory of catalogs and asked all the appropriate ones to carry it, we visited gift shops and asked them to carry the book. We even got gas stations, bakeries and restaurants to sell the book. It was a lot of effort—a minimum of 5 things a day, every day, day in and day out—for over two years.

Was it worth it? Yes! That very first *Chicken Soup for the Soul* book eventually went on to sell over 8 million copies in 39 languages. At a $1.20 royalty per book, it made Mark and I rich.

Did it happen overnight? No! We did not make the bestseller lists for more than a year after the book came out—a year! But it was the sustained effort of The Rule of 5 for over two years that led to the success—one action at a time, one book at a time, one reader at a time.

But slowly, over time, each reader told another reader, and eventually, like a slow-building chain letter, the word was spread and the book became a huge success—what *Time* magazine called "the publishing phenomenon of the decade." It was less of a publishing phenomenon and more of a phenomenon of unending persistent effort—thousands of individual activities that all added up to one large success.

What might you accomplish if you were to do five things every day for the next 40 years toward the accomplishment of your goal?

If you wrote 5 pages a day, that would be a total of 73,000 pages of text—or about 243 books. If you invested $5.00 a day at 6% interest, at the end of 40 years you'd have amassed a small fortune of $305,357.

Get Clear About the Steps
You Need to Take

A lot of people tell us their dream is to own a house in Hawaii or buy a yacht. While we're excited for them, we also have to ask them to get clear about all of the steps they'll have to take to get there.

Take buying a house in Hawaii, for example. You have to find out where the best locations are, decide which island you like, find out how much homes cost there, then determine how much money you'll need to save, where you can get your financing, where you'll get your furniture, how expensive that is...and on and on. Only then you can begin accomplishing these steps—5 a day until you achieve your goal.

Take Time to Plan How You'll
Practice The Rule of 5

While he didn't call it The Rule of 5, a seminar leader once said that, in order to arrive at the life of your dreams, you simply (1) make a wish-list of the activities, finances and lifestyle you'll be enjoying once you get there, (2) break down each wish on the list into the steps you'll need to take to achieve it, (3) choose a number of those steps to achieve each week or month or year, and, (4) achieve them.

Chapter Six:

Be Unstoppable in Your Giving

Tithing—that is, giving 10% of your earnings to the work of God, either through charities or through your church, synagogue or mosque—is one of the best guarantees of prosperity ever known. Many of the world's richest individuals and most successful people have been devout tithers. By tithing regularly, you too can put into motion God's universal force, bringing you continual abundance.

Not only does it serve others, but it serves you as the giver, too. The benefits cross all religious boundaries and serve those of every faith—because the simple act of giving creates both a spiritual alliance with the God of abundance, but also fosters the mindset of love for others. Tithing proves in a compelling way that abundant wealth is something God wants for his children. In fact, He created a world where the more successful you are, the more wealth there is for everyone to share. And according to economist Paul Zane Pilzer, an increase in wealth for an individual almost always represents an increase in wealth for society at large.

There Are Different Types of Tithing

As you advance along your success path, you'll need a tithing plan, just as world's wealthiest and most successful people have done.

Financial tithing is best explained as contributing ten percent of your gross income to your church, synagogue or that organization from whence you derive your spiritual guidance. Many successful people also tithe to their favorite charity— wherever your heart most compels you to help.

Time tithing is volunteering your time to serve your church, temple or synagogue, or any charity that could use your help. There are more than 18,000 charities in America alone that need volunteers.

In-kind donations are goods and services that you or your business can tithe to help a charity, church or other cause meet a goal—particularly when they can't afford the kinds of goods and services you can easily donate at little cost or expense to you. Workgroups at the office can hold a food drive for a local food bank or pantry. A Boy Scouts troop can bring paint, wood, and tools to build a storage building for a charity. And a bookkeeper can donate services to help a charity with their monthly accounting and reporting needs.

Finally, *idea tithing* is giving away your ideas for free. Charities benefit greatly when their Board of Directors, volunteers, donors and others contribute ideas, contacts, connections, and expertise the charity wouldn't otherwise have access to.

Meet the Authors...

JACK CANFIELD is the beloved originator of the *Chicken Soup for the Soul*[*] series, selling over 500 million books in 49 languages. He is America's leading expert in creating peak performance for entrepreneurs, corporate leaders, managers, sales professionals, corporate employees, and educators. Over the last 30 years, his compelling message, empowering energy and personable coaching style has helped hundreds of thousands of individuals achieve their dreams.

His latest bestselling book series is *The Success Principles*, coauthored with Janet Switzer and available in 36 languages. *Success Principles* trainings, coaching, and products are used by people in 112 countries. More than 3,500 people have been trained to teach these principles in over 100 countries.

DAVID MELTZER is the chief executive officer of Sports 1 Marketing, one of the world's leading sports and entertainment marketing agencies, which he cofounded with Hall of Fame Quarterback Warren Moon. Prior to Sports 1 Marketing, Dave was CEO of the world's first smartphone— the PC-E Phone—and later became CEO of the world's most notable sports agency, Leigh Steinberg Sports and Entertainment.

Dave is an award-winning humanitarian, an international public speaker, bestselling author, and is profiled by national publications such as *Forbes,* ESPN, Bloomberg, CNBC, Yahoo, *SB Nation* and *Variety.*

CYNTHIA KERSEY is the Chief Humanitarian Officer of the Unstoppable Foundation whose mission is to ensure that every child on the planet receives access to the life-long gift of education. Cynthia is also the bestselling author of two books in 17 languages, *Unstoppable* and *Unstoppable Women*, a collection of powerful stories and strategies from people who, through perseverance and consistent action, turned obstacles into personal triumph.

She's an inspiring speaker, a contributing editor to *Success Magazine,* and was featured on The Oprah Winfrey Show's television launch of the Angel Network. Cynthia's passion is showing how each of us can solve the world's most seemingly impossible challenges through simple individual actions.